MW01284601

How to Be A Good Employee

Easy Ways to Become a More Effective, Valuable & Higher Producing Employee

By
Kimberly Peters

Other Books
by Kimberly Peters

Relationship Kick Starter

How to Be a Good Manager

Contents

Introduction

When it comes to your career, most of us at least start out as an employee of some company. Many of us remain as employees for our entire working lives or careers while others might be bold and go out and start their own business. But whether we are a new hire or the Vice-President of a company, we are all employees.

If you have been in any workplace for a while you have noticed that there always seems to be a couple of people who just seem to move up the ranks and accomplish more in less time than the other employees. Though this sometimes is because of these individuals possessing off the charts great skills, the majority of the time skills are not the difference makers. In some cases, people with weaker or less developed skills are the ones moving past their higher skilled counterparts.

Though the reasons for this are many, the primary difference between those who stay at or near the bottom while others steadily grow in their careers is one of attitude and approach. In other words, those employees who steadily move forward in their careers do so because they have the right outlook and attitude when it comes to their future.

The good news for all of us that it is not difficult to create the right attitudes and behavior to become one of those "upwardly mobile" employees that steadily move forward with their careers. Though skills do play a significant role, this publication is going to concentrate on showing everyone what they can do to create a more positive image that will help them take advantage of more opportunities.

Some even better news is that these things can be learned and used by everyone no matter what position you currently hold or whatever industry you might work in. Even if you never held any kind of job and are just ready to enter the marketplace, we can help you. If you are re-entering the marketplace after a lengthy absence, we can help you as well. In short, there is NO ONE who will not benefit by the information contained in this book!

You don't have to spend any money to do most of these things and there is no prior education or experience required either. The only two things you are going to need to have are free and they are an open mind and some common sense.

You will need an open mind to understand the information and apply it in your life. You will need common sense to help you overcome some bad habits or thoughts you may already have now. If you have some common sense and an open mind you are all set to go.

Before we get started, let's discuss how this book is written and how you can get the most from it. Over the years we have learned that many people who read these kinds of instructional books do so because they have a specific or urgent need. Therefore they sometimes skip ahead to the parts of the book that pertain directly to their urgent needs. But by doing so, sometimes they might miss some information covered earlier to help them understand the latter portions of the book. This can create a problem.

To help solve that problem we have written this book in such a way that each chapter can be read as a standalone book. That means everything you need to understand the focus of that chapter is included in that chapter. The result is complete understanding without getting confused because something was left out.

But writing in this manner often requires that some information be repeated more than once within the entire book. That is because one piece of information might pertain to 2 or 3 different chapters. So if you see something repeated in the book this is not a mistake.

It is done for a reason. One other benefit of this is that repetition is one of the best ways to retain the information you have read. So not only do you understand the information better, you will retain it longer!

So feel free to skip around and read the areas that you feel might help you right away. Then, after you have done that, go back to the beginning and read the entire book straight through. The book is not long and reading it straight through will help you understand things better and retain it longer.

After each chapter take a break and think about what you just read and how you might apply it to your own career or situation. When you do this you help make the information more relevant to you. This helps add a dimension to your learning and helps bring the information "to life" in your brain.

After most chapters there will be a "How Do I Do This?" section that will give you specific ideas or thoughts on how you can take what you just read and integrate it into your own situation.

Try and use a few of those suggestions to help make things easier for you and to improve your chances for success. Not everything will be applicable to you so just use your judgment and pick the ones that make sense to you.

Feel free to take notes as writing things down also improves your comprehension and retention.

Use your own words and just don't copy things word for word. Putting it into your own words requires that you understand what you just read!

The Employee /
Management Relationship

Just like any relationship, the relationship between the employee and the company has two sides to it. It is not the responsibility of just one or the other party to make this relationship work. Both parties must be attentive and responsive in order for this relationship to grow and remain positive. It is not a 50%-50% responsibility but instead a 100%-100% responsibility.

What this means is that BOTH the company AND the employee has to make an effort to keep the relationship positive and growing. This is accomplished by doing several things. The employee has to keep a positive attitude towards the company and their job and how they do their job.

The employer must do their part to furnish a positive work environment and provide the employee with the tools and resources in which to do their jobs in a healthy and safe manner.

This does NOT mean that the employee or the employer must totally submit to the whims and demands of the other. When the relationship is no longer mutually beneficial and positive for either party the relationship may be terminated. The employee can leave for another job and the employer can terminate an employee for any number of reasons. But generally speaking, as long as both sides of the relationship are deemed mutually satisfactory, everything runs well.

One thing an employee must realize is that the employee is usually at somewhat of a disadvantage in the relationship because while the employee usually depends on their salary to feed and house their families, an employer can terminate an employee and replace them with someone else. Though there will be a learning curve during training and while the new employee learns, the company will survive.

Another part of the employee / management relationship is that rarely is it the case that someone is irreplaceable. While someone might be extremely talented and skilled, it is rare that a company will go out of business because one person leaves. So even though you might believe you hold the "upper hand" the fact is that most people can be replaced over time.

I tell you these things not to depress you or make you feel bad but rather because these are the realities of the situation.

The same holds true for the employers as well. For most employees there will be other jobs they can apply for, other companies they can work for, and other paths they can take if they become dissatisfied with their current situation.

It is important to understand these realities because it allows us to really understand the need and value of both employee and management working together to create a close and mutually beneficial relationship. Both management and employee must work together to resolve their differences and provide worth and value to each other.

If you look at the companies with the least amount of employee turnover you will see that those companies are the companies that treat their employees well. You will also see that the employees treat the employer well at the same time. It is only when that happens do employees remain with companies for long periods of time.

Part of any relationship also involves shared sacrifice. IN the case of the employee / management relationship that usually means working harder and longer when situations require it and also a commitment to the employee when times are slow or the economy is poor.

If the commitment between employee and employer is demanded to be just one-sided, then there is little hope for a long term relationship.

For example, employees are expected to do whatever is needed to get a project completed on time or an order fulfilled by a certain deadline. If the employees are not committed to accomplishing these goals, the company will suffer for it. Along the same lines, if the company places undo demands on the employees but let's people go at the slightest downturn in sales, that is wrong as well.

Loyalty and commitment is a two way street and the relationship between management and employee is a prime example of this. No employee should expect to be given everything and not give anything back and no employer should expect that as well. Shared sacrifice and shared rewards are the backbone of every employee / management relationship. It is from this that mutual respect and understanding is grown.

How Do I Do This?

Make an honest effort to see both sides of any issue or situation. Things are not usually as they might seem on the surface.

See what you can do to make things easier or better for your employer. It should not always be what they can do for you.

Treat your part of the relationship carefully and develop a certain level of respect for your employer. You should expect the same from them as well.

If you think the relationship is not worth it, remember you need a salary to feed your family and put a roof over their heads. While this does not mean you should subject yourself to poor treatment or abuse, it is none the less the economic reality of life for most people.

Goals of Employees

All employees have certain goals when it comes to their jobs or careers. They might be conscious goals or subconscious goals but they are goals none the less. Those goals are to get a job, keep their job, improve at their job and prepare for a better job. Depending on the stage of our career, that last one might cease to be a goal when we get closer to retirement.

Let's face it; we all want to get a job because we need money to live. We need to buy food to eat, provide clothing and shelter, medical care and to pay for the 457 channels we get on our cable or satellite TV box. Simply put, we work because we need money. Though we may love our job, most of us would not do it if it weren't for needing the money.

This is not meant to make anyone feel bad or to attach any negative connotation to our jobs and careers.

It is just to state that the reality of life is that most people work because they have to, not because they want to. A day spent at the beach or fishing or laying out back in a hammock usually ranks higher. But the point of this is to understand that we NEED to work.

We NEED to put up with certain things because no job is perfect and very few situations are perfect either. Our goal should not be to find a perfect job as much as it should be to find the best job. That means doing something we enjoy, something we are good at, close to home and at a nice salary. If we can hit all those, we have done a pretty good job.

Once we have a job, our primary goal is to keep that job. After all, we need to keep the job to keep money rolling in to pay rent and all those other expenses. One of the themes we will discuss throughout this book is the need to do certain things so that you will be able to keep your job and excel at it. The more valuable you can make yourself, the more secure your position with the company and in your industry will become.

Generally speaking, the employees most likely to escape a layoff or staff reduction are those employees that represent the highest overall value to the company. With that in mind we are going to teach you some strategies to help you increase both your real worth and your perceived worth. Both are important and we will show you how to accomplish both.

Our next goal should always be to constantly improve at our current job. That means improving skills, using our experience to do our jobs better and faster, and learning new skills to keep up with changes in products and technology. After all, you cannot continue to thrive tomorrow if you have yesterday's skills!

Employers want employees that perform at high levels and that are always interested in getting better at the things they do. They want employees who are not afraid to learn new things or grasp new technology. While you don't necessarily have to become an expert, you do have to be open to at least learning the basics. This is one goal that we never truly stop trying to achieve. That is because what you learn today might be outdated tomorrow so we have to always keep up with what's happening at our company and within our industry. It is always better to learn at your own pace now than to be forced to catch up later.

Last, but certainly not least. Comes our final goal and this is the goal many employees never think about or think about too late. That goal is preparing us for the next step in our career. This is another one of those processes that never really ends until we get close to the end of our career.

Even when we land a new or better job, we need to start thinking about what the next level or step is going to be.

Yes, you can celebrate and go out to dinner to toast your success and you can even spend some time getting used to your new position. But then you need to start working on what's coming up next and preparing for that.

We all follow these goals and we follow them in the same order. It is important to understand them because only when you understand them do you realize the importance of each one. If you understand the importance of having a job and why it is so important, you won't make the common mistake of quitting one job before you have another. If you understand each goal you will never allow an opportunity to go by because you never thought about the future and your place in it.

But there is another reason why every employee should understand these goals as well. That reason is that most employers or companies have those same goals for you as well. They want to help you with those same goals because as you benefit from them, so do they. Think about that for a moment.

When a company hires you, they hire you not only for what you can do for them today, but also what they think you might have the potential of doing for them in the future. They are not really interested in hiring someone for a position and have them stay in the same position for the next 30 years!

Instead they want someone that they can train and groom for advanced positions. As you improve (your third goal,) you become skilled and qualified for a better position (your fourth goal). This enables the company to promote from within and give better and higher paying jobs to people that they know and trust.

Most companies will ask you about your career plans. They want people who are aware of their goals and they want people who have a vision for not only where they currently are but also for where they want to be in the future.

If a company hires someone today it is because they feel that this employee has the ability to become the manager of tomorrow. They want to invest in their people so that as the employees grow, the company also grows.

Every employee should be aware of their goals and the importance of each one. Because when we understand the importance of something, we treat it with greater respect and are willing to put forth a better effort. We become more engaged and we become more productive.

At the same time we achieve each of our goals, we almost automatically increase our value in the marketplace and to our own company as well. This further helps us improve and get better and helps further increase our value.

But all of this only happens when we are aware of our goals and why each one is so important. Goals exist to help lead us to where we want to go in life. Whether it is to a new position or a new career, our focus must always be on where we are and where we want to be. We need a plan and we need focus. If we have those, everything else falls neatly in line.

How Do I Do This?

Create 1 year, 5 year and 10 year plans. Know where you would like to be every step of the way and what it will take to get you there.

Know where you are now and why you are there. Develop an appreciation for why you do what you do.

Always be pro-active. Take steps today to help prepare yourself for tomorrow.

Once you have your plan, consult it every month or at least twice a year to make sure you keep yourself, and your career, on track.

Always look for ways to learn more and improve.

Always look for ways to make yourself appear more valuable and important.

Understanding the Economics of Business

Though most employees do not wish to hear these things, it is important to understand the economics behind hiring an employee. Some people think that their salary is the only cost to the company and that everything else are just minor expenses. But the reality is that the entire compensation package usually is significantly higher than the salary alone.

Everything a company provides to its employees has a cost associated with it. Even things such as vacation time and sick time have costs attached to them. Whenever an employee is out they are getting paid but not producing any work for that day. So that work has to be done by others or wait until the employee returns. Delays mean money and this is no exception.

Extended absences may require reassignment of duties and responsibilities and the hiring of a temporary worker to take over until the employee returns. That cost may even be higher because of the temporary nature of the employment. So while many employees consider time off something that has value but doesn't cost the company a dime that is simply not true.

Medical care is a huge cost for the company and most employees pay a portion of their medical care as well. The employers share can amount to several hundred dollars a month or even more when family plans are involved. Medical costs are some of a company's highest employee related expenses.

In addition to all of these expenses, long and short term disability insurance, life insurance, retirement plan contributions, social security payments, and other company benefits provided at little to no cost by the company. Every one of these benefits comes with its own cost and that cost is at least partially paid by the company.

It is important to understand this because how much we are being compensated for doing our jobs has a direct influence on how we feel about our jobs and how much effort and commitment we will give to the company. This is not a conscious decision for some of us but rather human nature. The more value we see in something the more important we consider it to be in our lives.

For example, if you are an employee of a company and you make $50,000 a year, you might feel that you are underpaid in relation to the size of the company or the products it produces and your role in that production. You just cannot understand why you do not get paid more or get larger salary increases.

But the reality of the situation is that in addition to your $50,000 the company is paying another $20,000 in benefits bringing the total cost to the company for your position to $70,000 a year, not $50,000.

Benefits are an important part of the employee compensation package. For some people, benefits might be more important than their salary. For example, some people who work for universities receive free tuition for their children. In some cases that can amount to over $25,000 PER CHILD!

A common misconception of employees is that a benefit that costs the company very little to provide has very little value. Nothing could be further from the truth. IN the case of the college tuition above, it costs the college very little to provide that benefit. The seats are already there and it costs no more to teach 51 people than it does to tech 49. But even though the cost of providing this benefit is small to the company, it still represents a HUGE benefit to the employee.

Consider this, if you have two children going to college and you work at a university that costs $20,000 a year, that means the cost of sending each child through all 4 years would be $80,000!

For both children it would represent an AFTER TAX cost of $160,000 to send them to 4 years of college. When you factor taxes into the equation, you would have to earn over $200,000 to cover those expenses! So even though the cost to the university was minimal, the value to the employee would be off the charts.

We must ALWAYS figure out the value to US when we evaluate a particular benefit or compensation issue. This way we get a greater understanding of the true value of our job as it relates to US not the company. It makes no difference how much it costs the company but rather what it means to the employee that counts!

With all this in mind, the next time you think your salary is not appropriate for what you do and the value of the work you perform be sure to consider all aspects of compensation and not just your salary. Think about how it would be if you were self-employed and earning 25% more in salary but had to pay for medical and other benefits out of pocket. This is not to make you feel grateful or indebted to your employer but to just make you aware of that there are far more costs involved in hiring and employing someone than just the salary that employee is being paid.

So while you very well may be underpaid, your salary is not the only cost involved in bringing you on-board and keeping you with the company.

Be sure you consider everything when it comes to your overall compensation package.

There is one other misconception when it comes to salary and compensation. A lot of people, both in management and "regular" employees think that having a need for more money is a legitimate reason for deserving a raise in salary. There are some people who feel that if they are having a tough time meeting their financial obligations and paying their bills that they should get a raise in pay to help them live better. This kind of entitlement feeling is becoming more and more prevalent in today's society.

The reality is that in order to deserve a raise, you must be able to show that you are both entitled to the raise and deserving of one. Entitled to a raise means that your contract or employee handbook and company rules states that you are entitled to a raise for specific reasons. For example, if your company rules state that you are entitled to a 5% raise when you complete 5 years of service, then you are entitled to that 5% after you finish 5 years. You are entitled to it because you achieved a level of service. You do not get something because you FEEL entitled you get it because you ARE entitled to it.

For e the most part, salary increases are given for two other reasons. The most common are merit increases which happen at scheduled intervals usually once a year.

Your performance is evaluated and an increase is given according to established criteria. This is usually done for everyone at the same time.

On an individual basis, sometimes raises are requested by the employee. IN those cases, the employee must demonstrate why they feel they deserve an increase. Maybe they have taken on additional duties or responsibilities or maybe they have improved their value to the company. For example, they are now handling manager level tasks since their manager has been reassigned. Or perhaps they completed their college degree and have been doing advanced level tasks using their new knowledge.

In these cases, the employee should not just request the increase; they should prepare a "business case" for getting the increase. This would be a report detailing what they do, how it saves the company money or generates additional revenue and provides specific reasons why the deserve and have earned this increase. In simpler terms, this report or letter will give all the reasons why you should get the increase.

In some cases, when salary issues cannot be resolved you might be able to negotiate other things in place of money.

These other things might be additional vacation or personal days, the ability to work from home one or two days a week, additional contributions to your retirement plan or 401K or anything else you might place value in. For example, it might not be possible for you to get a $1,000 raise but your employer might agree to pay for some college classes or a membership to a local health club. Things like these might be able to be "buried" in a budget line somewhere without everyone else knowing.

That brings us to our last topic when it comes to compensation and the employee. For most companies, there are strict rules about how to compensate employees fairly and without discrimination. They might be limited in what they can do for an individual employee because they are legally bound to do the same for everyone. For example, they might not be able to give you a raise without giving 47 other employees that same raise. This protects everyone from discrimination in the workplace. This helps insure that everyone is treated equally and fairly and receives the same pay for the same work.

By understanding the economics of hiring employees and their overall compensation, you can better understand the full impact your presence has within the company. Knowing this will help you prepare a better business case and allow you to design a much better, and more accurate, approach to compensation issues.

You Have a Choice to Make

As an employee, or whatever role you might play in your career or company, you will always have a decision to make. You must make this decision every single day of you career whenever it comes up. Not only must you make this decision, you must also accept responsibility for your decision and not try to blame society or anyone else. It is you decision and you must accept the responsibility for it.

The decision you need to make is how you present yourself to the public and to your company and industry. You need to decide if you want to do what you want to do or what you need to do. Sometimes the decision is made for you and that happens when what you want aligns perfectly with what is needed or expected.

For example, you love getting dressed up in a suit and tie and you want to be a bank manager. Both lend themselves to each other perfectly.

But other times, what you want to do and what is need for you to do may be exact opposites of each other. When that happens, you have to decide which direction you want to go in. Do you want to do what is expected of you in order to get what you want or are you going to stay with what you want and try to take another route to your objective? Sometimes that decision isn't easy. For example, you might hate school but want to be a doctor. For example, you might love tattoos and body piercings but also want to be a financial advisor. I don't know many people who would trust their 401K or life savings to someone with a face full of metal and tattoos.

Some people feel very strongly that they should be able to go through life being true to themselves and their beliefs and values. While this is true to some extent, this right does not extend to everything in life. No one can discriminate against you because of your sex or religion but you cannot force any company to allow you to come to work in a Speedo or a thong!

While it is not fair in many respects, anyone work works in any capacity must understand that it is their responsibility to conform to what is expected if they wish to take advantage of all the opportunities that are available for them.

If they choose to be different and that is viewed as a negative, they must accept responsibility for that decision. It doesn't mean that decision is right nor wrong, it just means once you make it, you accept what comes from that decision.

For example, if you are applying for a job that requires 50 hours a week and you are only willing to put in 40, or if the job requires working the night shift and you only want to work the day shift, you cannot expect the employer to change the job requirements to suit your needs. They might be willing to if it makes sense to them but you should not expect it. They want what they want and if the employee wishes to get the promotion, they need to conform to the requirements not the other way around.

People must understand that career growth is a competition and employees are going to compete against each other for every promotion or new job that is out there. The "winners" are going to be those individual who best meet the expectations of the people doing the hiring or making the choices. Many factors go into these decisions and you need to decide what you are willing to do in order to be the winner.

That is not to say that you have to abandon your values or preferences. Sometimes the sacrifice might be too high. Only you can know when that is the case. If the sacrifice is too high, then you should walk away.

But if it means making some minor concessions in order to get something you really want in life, then you should consider making those concessions.

I often find it amusing that people feel the companies or society should conform to someone's individual choices. While that is a nice view, life just doesn't work that way. If you want something that someone else is offering to you, you must meet certain conditions for that offer to be made. If you don't meet those conditions, the offer goes to someone else. That's just how it works.

That may change as your career goes on and you get a reputation as one of the best in your field. As you get better and better known, other things become less important. But in the beginning, or until you get established, you have to decide if you are going to give people what they want or try and go it alone.

You may also decide that you are not going to conform to what someone else wants and because of that you will go it alone. Well, that is all well and good but you should be aware of one important thing: Whether or not you are self employed or working for someone else, you will need customers. Customers are going to do business with people they feel comfortable with and who inspire confidence. If you fit that mold you will do well.

But if you don't fit someone else's impression of what they are looking for, they will continue to look elsewhere whether you are self employed or working for someone else.

All of this is leading to one important question we need to ask ourselves. That question is: "Do we want to be right or do we want to be successful?" Many times you can do both but other times you will have to decide which path you want to take. You make the call and you accept the outcome.

Now that does not mean that you cannot try to change things once you are on the inside. Maybe you make a sacrifice in order to get hired and then once you get accepted on the "inside" you can start changing some of the corporate rules. For example, you might have to shave your beard to get a job but once you get it, you can work to change the policy against beards in the company. You might be successful and then again you might not.

We must make these decisions every day of our lives. Whether it is our business life or personal life, there will be crossroads where we will have to decide what we want to do. The answers might take us down completely different paths. Only time will tell but we have to make those decisions and then accept the responsibility for the outcome.

Again, let me state that no one should abandon their values and morals in order to land a job or a promotion.

People should always remain true to their core values and what makes them who they are. But there may be times when you may need to shift your ideals just a little bit to get what you want in life. In those situations, only you can know if that is the right path to take. No one else can make that decision for you. Only you will really know.

How Do I Do This?

Always ask yourself what you need to do in order to be the most successful at something. Then decide if you are willing or capable of doing each of those things. If you are, that's great. If you are not, it might be better to search out an alternative.

Discover what the expectations are for something before you make a commitment. If you are not willing to meet the expectations, move on to something else.

Search for careers and opportunities that most closely match who and what you are. This usually results in less change or adjustments.

Don't expect everyone else to conform to you. At times you need to conform to what others expect. Change may come later but not in the beginning.

The 3- Ps

We are going to talk about the 3 main parts of becoming a better employee and how to give the employee the best chance of career growth and success in the future. . It is a plan centered around three independent factors. Those 3 factors are Preparation, promotion and Performance. Everything we are going to do will fall in one of these 3 areas. All three areas are important and if you only do one or two of the 3, your results might suffer.

The great news is that anyone and I mean anyone, can easily master all 3 areas and easily implement them without any specialized knowledge, education or skill sets. If you approach your job and career with these three parts in your mind, you will be well on your way to both short and long term success.

We should also state as we have stated in a previous chapter, that these same 3 parts are the same things our employers look for when they evaluate their employees for performance and possible advancement. They want employees who think ahead and prepare themselves, improve their performance and make sure others know what they can do and are willing to do.

So that means employees who practice and follow this 3 part approach will be setting themselves up for more growth and more job security both now and in the future. It is a win-win for both the employee and employer.

Here are the three areas in our career advancement strategy:

Preparation

Sometimes the things we do that have the most benefit are the things we do to prepare ourselves for what lies ahead. That means doing things today that will prepare us and set us up for success tomorrow.

In the case of job hunting or furthering a career preparation might include obtaining the education, certifications or licenses you might need to move your career to the next level. It might mean spending time gathering information on the companies you are interested in working for or spending time today designing and improving your most current resume or updating an older one.

Another example of preparation might be taking a few practice interviews before going out on some real ones. Whatever you think might help you get ready for the next phase of your career would be examples of preparing yourself for the opportunities yet to come.

Promotion

If you want something in life you usually have to go out there and get it. It usually does not come to you! The only way you can get a better or new job is to put yourself in the best possible position to get it! IN other words, you have to make other people aware that you are interested and qualified for any opportunity that you are aware of.

That means you need to promote yourself, your skills, your talents and everything about yourself that will factor in to you getting a job offer. Self promotion, if done properly, will expose you to the people and organizations that are best able to help you get the job you want and help take your career in the direction you want it to go.

You can do the best preparation and perform at your very best as well but if people don't know about you they might never give you the opportunity to show them who you are and what you have to offer them. That is why self-promotion is so important when it comes to your career.

Performance

You can do your preparation and promote yourself to the best of your ability but all that will be for naught if you cannot perform when you need to. That means taking what is on your resume and demonstrating it to an interviewer or other people.

This is where many people fall short of expectations. People get scared or nervous and they freeze up or lose their nerve. Fortunately there are easy ways to deal with this and we will share them with you throughout this book. There is nothing to fear and eventually you will come to that understanding all by yourself.

Your ability to perform comes into play during interviews or phone conversations. This is one area where your preparation will help you craft the best answers to even the most difficult questions. This is where knowing what you are going to say before you need to say it will reduce stress and nervousness and allow you to do your best!

So these are the 3 P's that are going to help you get the job and the career you want for yourself. Please understand that these 3 processes work well when used separately as well as together. Preparing for anything is always a smart idea. Promoting yourself in the right way will get you noticed in your industry as well as bring you respect in the marketplace.

Last, but certainly not least, your ability to perform at your highest level will bring you the respect you need to convince people you are qualified and ready for bigger and better things.

But it is when we combine all 3 of these steps that they really come to work for you in a powerful way to bring you more success than you ever thought possible. It is a case where individual things come together to act even more powerful than they were individually.

It should also be mentioned that all three of these steps are never really finished. They continue to change and evolve as you change and evolve. There is always something new to learn about or prepare for and there will always be opportunities to promote yourself as well.

Never be satisfied to be where you are. Always look for ways to be better at something than anyone else. Always look for ways to make yourself more visible in your job, your community and your industry. And always practice your craft and strive to be the very best you can be in whatever you do. Never be satisfied by just being good enough. Always strive to be the best.

If you commit to all three parts of the process you WILL be successful. There is no doubt about that. But success means different things to different people. So take your time, watch the 3 P's and make a commitment to yourself to use all three parts and not just one or two.

As I said, if you do all three, you will be successful!

Taking Charge of Your Future

One of the great things about your job and your career is that you are in control of both where you are and where you want to go. While not everything will always go the way you want, and while there may be setbacks along the way, you will always be in charge of your future. That means you can go as far as you want and in the direction you want if you are willing to put in the time and effort.

But being in charge also means being responsible for where you are and where you are going. That means that YOU need to do what is required to get to where you want to be. You must not look for your boss or manager to plan out your career or hand you a promotion or a better job. That is something you need to go after not wait to have handed to you.

As we spoke already, every employee must have goals for the present as well as the future. Those goals will create a path for the employee to follow. But it is YOUR job to create those goals and YOUR job to follow the path your goals have set for you. Because this is your future, you have to be the o0ne taking charge and leading the way.

Your manager or boss should be part of that plan but they should not be expected to be the one guiding and pushing you. Managers sometimes have tens or hundreds of employees working for them and they just cannot be taking on the role or career counselor and personal career mentor. Yes, managers should develop their employees but they should never be placed in charge of an employee's future. That is the employee's job and no one else's.

Companies love to see employees working to better themselves. This shows character and personalities that are very highly desired in the workplace. So those employees who take an active role in making themselves better and more valuable in the workplace will get noticed by their employers at the same time.

Make no mistake, the employee should always be loyal to their job but they should be loyal to themselves first. Employees should strive to make themselves more valuable in the future so they are able to take advantage of opportunities wherever they should become available.

If they are in the same company then both employee and employer wins! But if the opportunity lies outside of the company, the employee should take advantage of those opportunities as well.

That is why it is important that the employee be in control of their future. If they allow their boss or the company's Human Resource people to guide their career, the only opportunities they will be exposed to are within that company. But when the employee takes control, then opportunities from all over are within sight.

Another important reason for the employee to take control of their own destiny and future is that they will always have their best overall interest as their main priority. A boss or manager, on the other hand, make like or appreciate an employee so much that they never want to lose them. So they may actively prevent those employees from moving up because they are afraid to lose them. Though this is not fair or right, it happens because while the employee will look after his or herself, the manager might place their priorities ahead of the employees.

My advice to any employee, no matter where they work or how long they work there would be to take charge of your future today. Not tomorrow or the next day but today. Ask yourself if you are where you want to be.

Enlist the help of people around you and solicit their advice. But don't let other people or your own company make decisions about your future. Those should be yours and yours alone.

If you are happy where you are and where your career is headed, then stay where you are and follow your plan. But if your current employer is not allowing your career to move forward, or if you have gone as far as you can go, do not stay just because you are comfortable. Go where you have the best possible chance of achieving your goals. That is where you should be at every stage of your life.

Education vs. Experience

One great way for employees to increase their value is to improve their skills and expertise. While there are several ways to go about accomplishing this goal, it is important to realize that we should take advantage of any way we can make ourselves better.

Employees should be viewing their job as a continuous competition. Those who do a better job or show more value are the employees that are offered the great rewards and opportunities. Education is one of the areas where anyone can make themselves better and more productive.

When most people think of education they think of colleges, universities and trade schools.

While these are the standard and most common forms of education, there are also other ways to gain the skills and expertise we need to increase or just maintain our performance in most industries.

Employees should look at education and expertise in two different ways. They should look at what they need to do what they are doing today and then they should look at what they will need to move ahead in their careers in the future. Failure to look at both goals can result in serious consequences.

Let's talk about what we need for today first.

In order to become well known and respected in our job today we have to be among the better performers. This is not something that we benefit in being in the middle group of performers. Our goals should be to be considered to be one of the best not one of the rest. Being the best means we are valued and appreciated on a higher level than most everybody else. This often can mean the difference between being safe in a layoff and being forced to look for a new job. It can also be the difference between getting that new job and coming in second or third.

Let's assume that you have, or at least had, the skills required to do your job at the required level when you were hired. Assuming that was the case, employees have the responsibility to keep their skills at the highest they can be.

That might mean taking classes, reading trade publications, attending seminars or perhaps getting some hands on training at the manufacturer or on site.

Most everyone will need to upgrade their skills from time to time. The very best way to do this is to be pro-active and improve your skills before it is needed. This way you can do this on your schedule and at your pace without being dictated to by anyone else. An added benefit is that as you upgrade your skills you usually improve your performance at the same time. That means you perform at a higher level faster than most everyone else. This will place you above most everyone else in the eyes of the company.

Another way to improve your skills is through employee sponsored training. Take advantage of any company training programs even if they are given after hours. If you have to take the courses on your time, remember that you usually do not have to pay for them out of pocket so that represents a considerable savings to you.

When you take advantage of company training, you not only get targeted skills you need in order to improve your performance, your manager and others in the company will be aware of your commitment to your job and the company. Companies look for employees who take advantage of opportunities to improve their skills.

So you not only get free training but you impress management at the same time! It is truly a win-win.

Now let's talk about improving you skills for the future.

As we stated before, companies look for employees who want to move up within the company. The problem is that some opportunities do not announce themselves until they become available. Because of this, the employees who act pro-actively and get the training and skills they need in advance are the ones who are usually more prepared to take advantage of opportunities when they arrive.

For example, let's say you want to become a manager and the qualifications include a certain type of certification. If you wait for the job to become available, you likely will not have the certification or be able to get it in time. So the result might be that you are not considered for the job or you will be passed over for someone who already has the certification. Either way, you will lose out on that opportunity.

But if you were pro-active and worked towards the certification now and completed that when an opportunity arrived you would be prepared while others are not. That means you can apply for the job, walk into the interview, and show them your certification and other qualifications. Having everything before you need it is the very best way to take advantage of everything that comes your way.

Many people don't like to do things until they have to. They will put in the effort to get the certification but only when they feel they need to. But consider what might happen if you don't get it and lose out on the job you want. Some people stay in their jobs for 5, 10, 15 or 20 years! So the job you just lost out on might not become available again for many years! Depending on where you are in your career, it may never come up again!

So let's all agree that it is in the best interest of the employee to take a pro-active approach as far as their careers are concerned. The next step is to know where you want to go and what it is going to take to get you there. Then you plan on how to get what you need for the next step so you will be prepared for everything when it comes.

We stated that education and experience can come in various forms. Here are some of the best ways to get the skills and expertise you need to succeed:

Classes

Taking classes to improve skills is the most common method of learning. You can take college or technical school level classes or even adult education classes. There are even manufacturers training classes you can get on specific skills or products.

Seminars

Seminars are a great way to get targeted or specific information in a day or two long class. Though sometimes relatively pricey, if you can get the company to pay the fees this can be a good way to get the skills you need. One downside is that these classes may only be held once or twice a year and you might have to travel to them.

Videos and Webinars

You can learn just about anything from a video or webinar today. Seminars are often given online through the webinar format. Some of them are live and interactive allowing you to ask questions just like you would be able to do in-person. Channels like YouTube may be of help when it comes to learning specific tasks or getting trained on some software or other skills.

Reading

There are books on just about every skill and subject. Books are good because they are always in front of you for use as a reference or guide. Plus, you can read them at your own pace so no one gets lost or left behind and no one gets bored because the class went too slowly! But be aware that some subjects might benefit from a video format where tasks and procedures can actually be shown and demonstrated.

On the Job Training

This can be one of the best ways to learn a new skill. You can work alongside someone who has the skills you want to learn and actually learn on the job. Ask you manager if you can shadow someone to learn how to learn something new. See if your company has a mentoring program where other employees teach their skills to other employees. The only caution I have on this approach is that sometimes you learn someone else's bad habits and not always learn the right ways to do things. On the flip side, learning from someone who has actually done it can give you special tips and tricks you will never get in a book or seminar.

Hands-on Training

When it comes to manual skills or tasks nothing, and I mean nothing, beats actually getting your hands dirty and doing it. You can read a book on computer graphics but once you actually create a logo or two you will really "get it". Once you have soldered a pipe or repaired a computer you will have the practical first-hand experience that is so critical for retaining information we learned.

Volunteering

If you want to learn something, go where that task or skill is being done and offer your time on a volunteer basis.

This way you can work alongside other people and learn from watching them and performing the task. This is the very same principle of apprenticeship programs. There are a lot of charitable organizations where you can learn skills and gain experience.

For example, if you are a clerk and want to move up to bookkeeper, learn the basics and then volunteer to do the books for a small company or organization. Not only will you gain valuable practical experience, you will have something to put on your resume or job application for actual experience!

Mentoring

Find someone you know that has the skills you want and ask them to mentor you. Use them as a resource to show you the right way of doing the task and to provide feedback and advice as you continue to learn. Work side by side with the person to learn all the tricks of the trade that only people who have worked at something for a long period of time will really know.

Experience

Practice makes perfect and doing something for longer periods of time will not only improve your skills but will also improve your speed as well. Being able to produce better results in less time is something that is in demand in every company and by every manager.

Plus, the more experience you can place on a resume or job application will make you appear more valuable and more desirable as an applicant.

Do not discount experience in the learning process. Some people learn by doing even though they may have little or no formal training. There are many self taught craftsmen and musicians for example. Just because you didn't take a class or read a book doesn't mean you cannot do something. Keep in mind that every single task we do today had to first be done by someone who had no training. Those people just figured things out as they went along. There is no reason why you cannot do the same.

No matter where you get the education and experience you need, just go out and get it. Getting it before you need it is always the preferable way to go. It is less stressful, prepares you much better for the future and allows you to take advantage of more opportunities that may come your way.

One more thing about education though. Education and knowledge are wonderful things. But they will do you no good in life if you don't use them. If you learn something new, implement it in your life or job, Use your new knowledge, apply it to what you do and practice, practice, practice.

This is how you turn knowledge into power and improve your skills, abilities and value in the marketplace.

This is how you make yourself more valuable than your co-workers and move to the top of the pack.

This is how you impress management, job recruiters and interviews.

This is how you take advantage of the best opportunities in life.

How Do I Do this?

Do a personal skills assessment and see how your skills stack up against others in your company. Upgrade weaker skills as required.

Ask yourself how old your skills are. When did you get your current skills? How have things changed since you were trained or went to school? This will give you a pretty good idea of where you stand.

Ask yourself what the next step should be in your career. Then find out what you need to do to prepare yourself for that step. Do this NOW rather than later so you will be ready when the next opportunity comes you way.

Expect More of Yourself

If you want to set yourself aside from most of the other employees and other people in life all you need to do is one little tiny thing. All you need to do is demand more of yourself than others demand of you. This might seem a simple thing to do and it is. But you would be shocked to know how many people refuse to do this very same thing!

The world is full of people who do what they are told or asked and not a single thing more. If they are asked to do A, B and C they do A, B and C even though they know that D, E and F need to be done as well. If they are expected to complete a task in 20 minutes they do it in 20 minutes even though they believe they could do it in 15 if they put their mind to it.

In other words, the world is full of people who believe that doing something "good enough" is good enough. Being able to demand more of yourself will automatically raise you above almost everyone else because you will push yourself to do things better, faster and with better results. Not because you were told to or expected to but because you can and because you want to.

An added benefit of adopting this attitude is that it takes the pressure off achieving goals assigned to you at work. That's because if you assign yourself a personal goal that is higher or more difficult to achieve and you achieve that personal goal, you automatically achieve the assigned goal! You don't have to work towards THEIR goals; you just have to achieve YOUR goals.

Every year I look at what people expect me to do and compare that to what I KNOW I am capable of. Then I create my own list of personal goals and work towards achieving those goals. I don't forget about the assigned goals because they are still there. But since I know that if I work at my goals I automatically achieve the others, it makes everything easier!

I believe that I should always try and do my best. It's just the way I am but it has worked out well for me and it can work out well for you too. The reason it works well is that you become accustomed to demand more of yourself.

You will find yourself spending a little more time, concentrating just a little bit more and producing even better quality of work. You will finish something, look it over, and decide you can do better. You will not be tempted to submit something because it is good enough. You will submit it because it is up to your standards not theirs!

This does not mean you have to become a perfectionist and obsess over every detail and never be satisfied. That attitude just brings frustration. Instead, you demand better results and a better effort from yourself because you know you are capable of it. You don't have to be perfect or expect to be perfect, you just have to expect more from yourself than others do.

Another thing happens when you adopt this attitude. People recognize the quality of your efforts and your commitment to quality and excellence. You become the person known for producing quality results that exceed most everyone else. You become the "go to" person in your office when things have to be done and be done right.

When review time comes around and you have hit every goal and have become known as someone who consistently produces the best results, you will be sitting there in a position of strength. When you apply for that promotion you will be someone who is considered at the top of their peers and receive more consideration than most everyone else.

You will achieve this not because you are necessarily the smartest or most skilled or because you have the best education. You will be in that position because you did one little thing the others simply refused to do. You just expected yourself to be better than what others expected.

And that's a pretty smart approach to just about anything in life.

Do MORE Than
What is Asked!

We just finished discussing how improving our knowledge and keeping our skills current will help set us apart from the rest of the pack. Phase two of developing a great employee attitude is trying to go above and beyond and do more than what is asked of you. This will help establish you as an employee who is committed to doing a good job and also being committed to doing what is best for the company.

We also stated that the world is full of people who go through their days doing as little as they possibly can. We all know the type because we all have worked with them. These are the folks who feel content to sit at their desks or stand by the coffee station or water cooler and wait for someone to find them and ask them to do something.

Some of these individuals spend more time and effort avoiding work than they do actually doing work!

Companies and managers look for people who are not afraid to work. They want people who will be willing to do something that needs to be done even though it technically might not be their job or responsibility to do it. In other words, they are looking for people who will do what needs to be done without having to be asked or tracked down.

Companies value employees who are team oriented and look to help first and do what needs to be done without trying to figure out if it is their responsibility first. Companies look for employees who will step up rather than step away. They appreciate the "can do" attitude and look for that in employees they are thinking about moving up within the company.

Sometimes company policy or union rules and regulations prohibit people from doing the things that they are willing to do. But there should always be room for someone who wants to do more than their fair share and for those employees who just want to help out and do the right thing.

Are you going to be one of those employees?

How Do I Do This?

Look for ways to help instead of waiting to be asked.

Look for value added things you can do to help the office or company.

If something needs to be done, see if you can do it first before you ask someone else to do it.

If something needs to be done and the person who usually does it is not available, volunteer your expertise if you have it.

If deadlines become tight, ask what you might be able to do to help. Even if there is nothing you can do, the gesture will be noted and appreciated.

Do What Others Will Not Do!

In every office and every company there are tasks or responsibilities that no one really wants. Maybe it is a horrible shift or a really dirty or disgusting task. Perhaps it is something basic that some people feel is "beneath their pay grade" to do. Whatever these tasks or assignments might be, your willingness to do them will give you exposure you need and a reputation of being willing to help out wherever and whenever needed.

If you look at the life stories of some of the most successful people in this world you would see that in their early days they did some pretty basic and down and dirty tasks. They looked for services and products no one else wanted to produce and they provided them. They looked for ways to separate themselves from the rest of the people.

They were not afraid of being ridiculed or made fun of because of what they did or how dirty they got. The paid no attention to people who made fun of them because they did low paying jobs that no one else wanted to do. Instead, they did those jobs and created their own little "niche" in the system. They quickly became a positive influence within the company and rose through the ranks.

I'm not saying that you have to volunteer for every graveyard shift or take the weekend overtime on Super Bowl weekend every year. But when it is convenient and when you are asked, step up and take the bad shift or do the menial task and do it with a smile on your face. Every time you do something small you make yourself look bigger. Every time you help out while everyone else goes home, you become known as a more valued employee.

Now this does not mean you should do something that everyone else refuses to do because it is dangerous or unsafe. Naturally your own safety should be your main concern. The same goes for illegal activities. If people refuse to do something because it is against the law, you should refuse to do it as well. But when it's just something dirty or inconvenient or messy, shove your pride and ego aside and just go help out once in a while. You never know who will see you and notice what you are doing!

This is something pretty basic that everyone can and should do from time to time. So the next time there is something that no one else wants to do, why not consider stepping up and showing that your focus is on your job and the company not on your own pride and ego.

You might be surprised where this attitude can take you.

How Do I Do This?

It's easy. Just do something that needs to be done that no one else will do. It's not rocket science!

Learn What the Boss Wants!

Everyone is different and everyone wants different things or wants things done a certain way. As an employee, it just makes sense to learn what the boss wants and expects and then do your best to provide that to them when asked. It's not a big thing and it should be common sense, but a lot of employees fail to grasp the importance of doing this and it can cause problems.

The best employees take the time to understand what their boss likes and how he or she likes it. Then they make it a priority to adjust their own way of doing things to match the needs of their boss. It is a simple concept but despite the simplicity of it, many employees just keep doing things the way they want to do them!

Doesn't it make sense that if you, as the employee, does things more like the way the boss wants them done that your boss or manager will think more highly of you than other people? If you do things in the manner which the boss wants them, and the boss has to correct you less, talk to you less, and just knows he will get the best results from you, isn't that exactly what you should do?

For example, if your boss likes employee reports done during the first part of the week and he wants them on white paper with the data last and the explanation first, why can't you do the reports in that manner. If you hand in the report on Thursday and on yellow paper with the data first, all that will tell the boss is that you either don't listen or you don't respect his or her wishes. Neither is a really good idea to plant in the bosses mind!

Even though you might not be aware of why the boss wants something the way they want it, you should follow their direction. In the case of the above report, maybe the boss has to take 15 reports from 15 different individuals and bind them together to form a multi-departmental report. That is why the boss wants them all on the same color paper and in the same format with the explanation first and the data second. This way the report will read uniformly all the way through.

The best employees do the best job they possibly can and they follow rules and processes as closely as possible. They can question something if they don't understand it but when push comes to shove, they follow procedures and protocols. In other words, they do what they are supposed to do.

Think about how you want things done for you. Do you want people to follow your instructions and give you things the way you like or do you just accept things the way others want to do them for you? You probably want things done a certain way for reasons maybe you only know.

Like so many other things in life, if you want something a certain way for a certain reason, it stands that other people might feel the same way. So treat your boss or manager with respect and respect what they tell you to do and how they tell you to do it. Even though you may not be aware of the reasons behind the request, you should respect the request itself enough to follow the rules and procedures.

How Do I Do This?

Listen carefully to instructions. If any are unclear, ask questions to clarify anything you are unsure of.

If written instructions are available, keep a copy of them and refer to them before doing the task.

If no instructions are provided but you have done the task in the past, ask if it should be done the same way as last time.

If in doubt, ask!

Observe the boss or manager to get a better idea of what they want and expect from the employees. Use that to help decide how things should be done moving forward if no specific directions are provided.

Really Listen

One of the skills that will help us greatly over the course of our life is the ability to really listen to what others are saying to us. Not just listening but REALLY listening. Really listening requires hearing just the words. It means hearing the words and the emotions and meaning behind the words. Only when we hear all the components in what people are saying can we totally understand what they are trying to tell us. This is important in every part of our lives not just at work.

On a very basic level, we need to listen effectively to avoid confusion and missing all or part of what is being said to us. The more we understand what we are hearing the better and more accurate the decisions we make will be. It is when we have to "fill in the blanks" with what we "think" we heard that problems arise.

For example, suppose your boss says to you, "Make sure to get the Cohen report done by Friday and fax it over to their offices. Make sure to use a 10% profit margin and not the 5% we originally talked about." There were three instructions in that request. Do the report by Friday, fax it to the client and use a 10% profit margin not the 5% that was originally discussed.

What might happen if you "heard" only two of the three instructions? What if you were not really paying attention because you had done this 50 times before and the process was always the same? What if your mind "zoned out" because you had heard this all before several times?

Well, maybe you completed the report by Monday and the client already made their decision based on the reports he received on time. You might have lost a deal or contract because you were late.

Or maybe you did the report on time and left it on your manager's desk instead of faxing it and he was out of the office until Wednesday of next week and the report just sat on his desk and never made it to the client? That could cost you the deal or contract as well!

Last, but certainly not least, what if you used the 5% profit margin because that was what you had discussed up to the point and did not change things to reflect a 10% margin?

You would get the report done in time, fax it to the client on time and they would be getting on heck of a deal because you cut the profit margin in half! That could end up costing your company thousands or millions of dollars. Plus, a mistake like that could possibly cost you, and possibly others, your jobs!

Employees are expected to listen to what they are being told and to perform tasks in the manner that they are told. They are expected to follow their instructions 100% of the time without fail. That is not because they are employees but because that is what people in any capacity inside and outside of business are expected to do. They are expected to do what they are asked to do, in accordance with the instructions they are given, 100% of the time. Not 50% or 80% of the time but 100% of the time.

That means you must learn how to listen effectively. While entire books have been written about listening skills, here are a few short points you should consider when it comes to listening both in the workplace and outside the workplace:

Don't Multitask When Listening

One of the most common reasons for not hearing everything that is being said is that people try to do other things when someone is talking to them.

They might be typing something, doing research, watching something on TV or a myriad of other things.

When you try to do more than one thing at a time, you cannot possibly give your total attention to anything. Your brain is always switching back and forth paying attention to everything you are doing. This might cause you to miss words or even entire sentences! This is especially true if you are trying to carry on two separate conversations at the same time!

When someone is talking to you concentrate on that conversation. Pause the TV, put down the pen, and leave that spreadsheet for a while so that you can concentrate on the conversation. This will enable you to better understand the full content of the conversations and not just bits and pieces.

Pay Attention to Who is Speaking

Most of us fail to really pay attention to people when they talk to us. Maybe we are preoccupied with other thoughts or maybe we just don't care for the person doing the talking. Sometimes we just are not interested in the topic of the conversation. We might have heard it a thousand times before and are sick of hearing it.

Whatever the reason, we need to force ourselves to pay attention so we hear everything that is being said and so that we do not miss an important word or bit of information that could be important later on. Just like the 10% profit margin we used in the previous example. Just miss that and a huge mistake will follow!

Reduce Distractions

Distractions can really impact our ability to hear and process everything that is being said. Not only does it make it difficult to hear the words being spoken, it interferes with your ability to hear the emotions behind those words. That can be a critical component in the conversation.

Noises, other conversations, whine from machinery or construction are just a few of the common distractions we might encounter in the workplace. Care should be taken to hold important conversations, if not all conversations, in a place where it is quiet and free of distractions. This will enable everyone to hear all parts of the conversation easily and accurately.

Separate Emotions

The emotions behind the words we speak are sometimes a critical part of the conversation.

Angry or upset people will say things they really might not mean and they may overstate or distort the truth in the process. As a rule, angry people make very poor communicators. The angrier a person is the less accurate their conversations are likely to be.

Emotions can also give us an indication of how serious a situation really is. When something is delivered in a very serious or somber manner, we might want to make sure we hear everything as this might be a very critical or serious request with a lot at stake.

Emotions and other non-verbal clues in the conversation actually deliver more content and information than the words we choose. In a normal conversation, less than 10% of what we communicate comes from the actual words we use. The other 90+ percent comes from emotions, body language and expressions. So be sure to fully concentrate on the emotions behind the words to get the full impact of what is being spoken.

Watch for Visual Clues

OK, we just told you that less than 10% of what is communicated to us comes from the words that are used. The rest comes from emotions and body language and facial expressions.

How a person looks and acts while they are speaking gives us some insight into how the other person is feeling at that particular moment.

Facial expressions will indicate if someone is angry or sad or happy and pleased. They will indicate when something is important or when something is trivial. It is important to understand these things so the proper response to the request is understood.

Body language refers to how a person presents his or herself during the conversation. If they are up in your face and leaning forward suggests the person is angry and looking for a confrontation. If they stay back in a relaxed stance they are most probably content and relaxed. How a person stands in relation to you can provide a huge amount of insight into how they are feeling at that particular moment.

Always take notice of facial expressions and body language of the other people in the conversation. Those clues, along with the emotions behind the words and the words themselves will help you more clearly and accurately hear what is being said in any conversation.

Don't Think You Know What is Going to Be Said

How many times have we jumped to a conclusion and stopped listening because we thought we knew what was being discussed and what the rest of the conversation was going to be?

If you are like just about everyone else, you do that quite often. After all, if your boss tells you every week to do the same thing the same way, eventually you are just going to assume he is telling you the same old thing yet again. So we zone out and jump to conclusions.

The danger in this is that sometimes little things change. Sometimes big things change as well. Maybe the way a report is done will change or a different form should be used. Maybe figures need to be updated. Maybe a profit margin needs to be changed from 5% to 10%! Whatever changes need to be done will be conveyed in the conversation. If you stop listening, you stop hearing.

One of the most common situations like this is when a customer comes to you with what you view as a common complaint. You rush to the conclusion and don't really continue to listen. After all, 50 people have made the same complaint and it was always the same problem, right?

Well, when we jump to conclusion we either interrupt the customer or zone out and we might miss some other bit of information that would lead us down a completely different path to another possible problem. The result is that we resolve the wrong issue and the problem often continues for the customer.

Never feel that you know what is going to be said before it is said. Keep an open mind and listen until you have all the information that is available. Only then can you make proper and accurate decisions that are based on all the information not just selected parts of it that you really heard.

Don't Be Afraid to Speak Up

When you are really listening and something doesn't make sense to you or is even the slightest bit confusing, ask the appropriate questions so that everything is clear to you and everyone else. This will help you avoid mistakes and wasted time. These often occur when people "connect the dots" with what they think instead of what they really know. Ask the questions that need to be asked until you are sure of what you are to do.

If you cannot hear what someone is saying because of noise and other distractions, speak up. Chances are if you cannot hear the conversations others will be having the same problem. If it is hard to listen it is also hard to comprehend!

If something doesn't make sense to you, it is possible that you considered something that someone else did not. In those cases raise the question and bring up what you think is wrong. Do it tactfully and not in a confrontational manner.

You focus should not be on placing blame for the mistake but rather to make sure everything is done proper with the best possible result.

Listening is one of the most important skills any employee can have. Proper listening skills reduce errors and mistakes, reduce wasted time and resources and allow everyone to function at a higher level. This results in higher productivity and less stress in the workplace.

Are you listening to all of that? Or just some of it??????

How Do I Do This?

Concentrate on the conversation and nothing else. Do not multi-task!

Hear the words and the emotions behind them. Only then can you hear everything!

Use your eyes as well as your ears when you listen.

Eliminate or minimize distractions so that everyone can hear what is being said.

If you cannot understand the person who is speaking, tell them nicely to speak more clearly.

Learn from Your Mistakes

One thing every employer and employee realizes, or at least should realize, is that people are going to make mistakes. Managers, CEO's and employees are all going to make mistakes. You cannot eliminate mistakes but you can take steps to minimize them. Plus, there is one important thing everyone can do when it comes to their mistakes.

They can learn from them.

If you think about mistakes for a minute, you will see that mistakes usually come from a lack of experience of knowledge. This is not always a negative because no one should be expected to know everything. But as we go through every day and experience new things and learn new technology, we are bound to make mistakes throughout the learning process.

While some mistakes come from carelessness or laziness, the majority are what we will refer to as "honest mistakes". Honest mistakes are things we do with good intentions and expectations but don't turn out the way we intended when we did them.

A perfect example of making mistakes through the learning process is a baby trying to learn how to walk. You and I walk without thinking because for us, we have had practice and we have learned how to step and balance ourselves at the same time. While we can run and turn and jump, a baby has trouble at first just standing. They stand, wobble a bit and fall down. Then they stand longer and longer until standing is not an issue.

Then they take a step and fall and they try again and again. Then one step becomes two steps, two steps become three and eventually the baby is running all over the place and the parent's life takes a permanent turn in the future!

When the baby was falling it wasn't because the baby was careless or lazy or liked the feeling of smashing his or her head on the carpet. It was because they were trying something new and they had to learn. But the baby did what all of us should do when we make mistakes. The baby took a step, fell and then learned that was not the right way to walk.

So they made a little change in their step and things got better. They continued to make adjustments and eventually they were walking and running like the rest of us.

Employees are going to make mistakes. Good managers understand this and even expect it. New employees probably will make more mistakes than older employees because they lack the experience other employees have. But the issue here is not whether or not we will make mistakes but instead what we will do once we make them.

First and foremost, when you make a mistake, admit it and take ownership and responsibility for it. Do not look to hide it or run away from it. When we accept responsibility we show others we are responsible and we tell ourselves that we need to change what we did for next time. When we accept responsibility for our actions and take the consequences we are far less likely to make the same mistake again in the future.

And that is exactly the point. Good employees will make mistakes but they will learn from them and not make the same mistakes over and over again. Other employees, who refuse to learn, or make no attempt to learn, will continue to do the same things over and over and over again and make the same mistakes over and over as well. That is precisely what drives managers and employers crazy!

A good employee will take a mistake and tear it apart to see where they went wrong. They will look for things they could have done differently or something that should have been done better or even not at all. They will look at a mistake every step of the way to see how they might handle things differently next time.

They will seek out the advice of others to explain why something did not go as planned and learn from their expertise. In other words, good employees will do whatever it takes to learn from their mistakes so they can improve their knowledge and expertise and avoid making the same mistakes again.

Really good employees, usually those with a high degree of self confidence, might also consider making others aware of what has happened and explain it to them so they might avoid the same mistakes as well. This can happen at staff meetings or perhaps by reporting it to the manager so he or she can make others aware. This way everyone benefits from your experience.

How Do I Do This?

If you make a mistake, acknowledge it and accept responsibility.

Break down what happened and see where you went wrong. Discover where the error was made, why it was made, and how you can avoid it in the future.

If the error came from a shortage of knowledge, take steps to improve your knowledge.

If the mistake was due to poor or lacking skills or expertise, improve your skills and expertise in the future.

If others are likely to make the same mistake, let them know what happened and what you did to prevent a reoccurrence.

Turn every mistake into a teaching opportunity.

Leave Your EGO
at Home

If you really want to be a great employee, and be looked upon favorably and positively by management and others in the workplace, consider leaving your ego at home when you leave for work every day. No one likes someone who feels and acts like they are better than everyone else in the office. Even if that is the case, employees do not need to act as if they are.

People who are confident in their abilities are the people who do not come off as being better than everyone else. Instead, they allow their performance and actions speak for them. This doesn't mean that they do not take charge when needed or do the things they need to do in order to be successful. It just means they go about it in a quiet and reserved manner.

People who continually feel the need to brag and profess them to be the best usually aren't the best. They are insecure and are trying to convince others that they are better than they really might be. In some cases they might try to look better by making those around them look worse. We all know the type. They make the mistakes and blame others. Or when others make mistakes they make sure everyone knows about them.

Ego's also sometimes get in the way of getting things done. An inflated ego might lead some people to refuse to do things or participate in things that they consider "beneath them" even if those things really need to be done. After all, someone needs to do those tasks and who is to say that one person is any better than someone else?

The employee who is appreciated more and who grows faster within the company is usually the person who has the skills and expertise and uses them to get the best results. They will take credit for what they have done when it is deserved but they will usually spread the credit around to those who deserve it.

They will also make a great effort to work with others to get things done without particular caring about who gets the credit. They will do things because they need to be done not because they will look good or bad doing those things. Sometimes just the fact that a person is willing to do something speaks louder than any bragging or demand for recognition.

Egos are good when it comes to gaining the confidence in our abilities. They help us be assertive and also help us become leaders when the situation calls for leader ship. But ego's can also cause us to behave in such a manner as to alienate the people and workers around us as well. Sometimes it is a delicate balance that must be carefully monitored at all times.

Egos should also not demand to be treated differently than other people or receive special attention. All employees should adhere to the same rules and policies as everyone else. They should not be allowed to do things that other employees are not unless there are really good reasons for doing so.

Use your ego to help you go through life and do the things you want to do. But do not allow your ego to take over who you are and how you act. Do not allow yourself to become conceited or overbearing with other people. One of the best skills employees and other people have is their ability to get along with others. If you demonstrate that you feel superior to everyone else you will not get the recognition or opportunities that your skills and expertise deserve. When that happens your ego will be the reason why.

How Do I Do This?

Don't feel that you are better than anyone else. You can feel more skilled but not better.

Strive to be one of the team on an equal footing not someone who demands to be treated better or differently.

Share the credit when that is appropriate. Do not take all the credit when things go right and hide when things go wrong.

Do things because it is right to do them. Do not do things because they will advance your personal agenda.

Help others when they need it. Do it anonymously and do not expect or seek out credit or recognition.

Do not Whine
or Complain

No one likes people who whine and management are no different. Management loves employees who see things that need to be done and go ahead and do them. They love to see employees fix something that needs to be fixed or made better. What they don't like to see are employees who just whine and complain and then walk away.

There is not an office or company in existence where everything goes right all the time. Some might come close but there will always be problems and situations that make some people angry or upset. Things will go wrong, something will break or cease to do what it is supposed to and people will leave or get sick or cause problems. It happens in every office and inside every company.

The key is not to make everything perfect because that is impossible. What should be the focus is what to do when problems do occur. Employees play an active role in every office. In many cases employees may cause or at least contribute to problems and certain situations. So when problems occur, good employees are the ones who look for solutions and ways to make things better. They do not just complain and complain about things. They do something about it!

We all have worked with the employee who just walks around and finds fault with everything in the company. The hours are too long, the management is unresponsive, the office is too hot, the music is too loud, the water cooler is not cold enough; the bathrooms are dirty, etc, etc. After a while you just get tired of hearing the constant stream of complaints.

The best way for employees to deal with situations or problems is to try and understand the cause of the problem and then either figure out a solution or learn to deal with it more effectively. If you must bring it to someone's attention, try and accompany the complaint with a possible solution or two. That turns the focus off the negative and brings it into the positive. The complaint turns into a solution that helps make things better.

For example, if the temperature in the office is too cold, you might say something to your boss like this:

"The office is too cold in the winter because we always leave the door open. If we could keep it close when it's really cold outside that might help." That type of complaint shows that thought went into a solution and that you are not complaining just for the sake of complaining about something.

Sometimes a complaint will deal with a legitimate issue caused by a company policy. In those cases, the employee might suggest a change in policy to help address the problem. For example, the employee might say something like "I know we are supposed to wear a collar and tie in the office but it gets so hot in here in the summer maybe it would be possible to change the policy to make the tie optional in the summer?" That sound much better than going to the boss every single day and saying "Jeez, it is always so freaking hot in here! I'm going to pass out one of these days!"

The same approach can be made when dealing with issues between employees as well. Most managers are too busy to step in and mediate every single disagreement between employees. Using the same approach can help make things better for everyone in the office. For example, if one employee plays music too loud, you might say something like "I know you like to listen to your music but it distracts me from doing my work.

Do you think you could either turn it down a little bit or maybe wear headphones? That way I can work and you can listen to your music."

A more diplomatic and positive approach to complaints will usually yield much better results for both employees and management. Always try to accompany a complaint with a possible solution or two. This shows thought and a desire to make things better and not just be a person who just likes to complain.

How Do I Do This?

Always try and accompany a complaint with a suggested solution.

If you see something that can be made or done better, don't just complain, do something about it.

Be pro-active when it comes to complaints. Do something today to prevent a problem tomorrow.

Try and maintain a positive outlook on most everything. Everyone around you will appreciate that.

Don't complain about the little stuff. Learn to let the little stuff go. This way when you do complain people will listen and not just say to themselves "Oh. No, not another complaint!"

Step Up!

Just a quick hitter here for those employees who want to make a great impression on their boss or manager. When your boss has something that needs to be done, instead of waiting to be picked, why not volunteer instead?

A lot of people go to work hoping and praying that they are not given any more assignments or things to do. They hide I the corner, avoid eye contact with the boss, head for the bathroom when they see the boss coming and anything else they can think of to avoid work. These are the same people who always complain that they are too busy to tackle anything else at the moment.

Most of the time the other employees and management are aware of what these employees are doing but sometimes it really does go unnoticed. That is, until someone brings it to the attention of the boss. But the employee who volunteers for projects or tasks is almost always noticed by the boss!

From a manager's point of view it is great when someone volunteers to do something. When that happens the boss does not have to assign the task to someone who may already feel overwhelmed or just doesn't want to do it in the first place. Most of the time when someone asks to do something it is something they enjoy and that almost always results in a better effort with better results.

Another benefit to volunteering for something is that you will get to do more of the things you like or are good at. For example, if your boss has something that needs to be done that you enjoy doing, volunteer for that and you will likely be able to avoid the next request which might be something you don't like at all! So while you might take on more work right now, it will be work you enjoy and the other stuff just might go to someone else!

This is an extension of the pro-active philosophy where we take control by seeking out what we want to do. We provide the boss with someone who will do what they want and that makes their life easier. You get to do more of what you enjoy and that makes your life easier as well. Not only that but you get the reputation of being cooperative and helpful. You get the reputation of being a team player and being a positive influence on others.

Like most everything else in life you should use moderation in volunteering.

Don't be a "hog" and take every request that comes along. Don't be seen as "kissing up to the boss" or anything like that. Just take control and volunteer whenever you feel it will be helpful. Give other people the chance to do the same when something comes up that you know they will like or be good at.

This is all part of working together to achieve common goals. Volunteering for things will give you visibility to management and will stand to make everyone else happy at the same time as long as it is done with moderation.

How Do I Do This?

If the boss has an assignment, volunteer for it before it is assigned to someone.

If you know something is going to need to be done, act proactively if it is something you would like to do. Ask your boss or manager if they would like you to do it.

Always do a good job on assignments you request so the response will be favorable next time as well.

If an assignment comes up that you know other people usually like, step back and give them a chance to volunteer before you do. If no on steps up, it is fair game for you or anyone else.

Do not volunteer for something if that extra workload will negatively impact your standard duties or responsibilities. Always think of workload before committing to any extra work.

Keep track of extra work you have done over the year in case you are up for a promotion or salary review.

To Be or Not to Be?

This part of the book will deal with the character traits and actions that are most desirable and looked for in employees. You already probably possess some or all of these traits but if you don't consider each one of them. Remember the idea is to become the very best employee that you possibly can be.

Implementing each or all of these traits is not difficult and can be done by anyone with very little effort. The result will help you become someone who is looked upon more favorably and positively by everyone around you.

As you read this section, please do not feel insulted or marginalized in any way. We are going to explain things from a management point of view and how they view their employees.

When you look at things from a management point of view, they might see things differently as employees see them. That does not make employees any less valuable to the company. All this means is that we are looking at things from a different point of view.

That right there should be reason enough to read this part of the book!

Be Low Maintenance

Employees are the responsibility of the manager. That means that the manager is accountable for everything pertaining to his or her employees. That means performance, issues, problems, questions; productivity and many other things pertaining to the employee are the responsibility of the manager.

Multiply that by the number of employees that a manager is responsible for and you have the potential for an endless stream of tasks for the manager. That is in addition to his other responsibilities the manager is responsible for. So the employee needs to understand the benefit of being as low maintenance as possible.

Being low maintenance means not constantly being someone the manager has to interact with or deal with as far as problems or issues are concerned.

The less interaction you require on a daily basis, the more valuable you will become to that manager. The more you require the manager's attention, the less valuable you will be in the eyes of the manager.

For example, let's say that a manager has 50 employees that he is responsible for. If every employee required just 5 minutes with the manager each day that would mean the manager would spend 250 minutes, or 4 hours, or half their work day just answering questions or dealing with employee related issues. So it is not a case of the employee's issues not being valuable or important to the manager, it is a case of simply not having enough time in the day to deal with every little thing. It's not that the manager doesn't want to spend this time with the employees; it's just that he can't.

Great employees know what they should be doing and go about their business without causing any problems or issues. They follow procedures, do what they are told and follow instructions carefully and completely. In other words they go about their day requiring very little input, correction or instruction.

Great employees don't cause problems. IN fact, they do exactly the opposite. They see problems and they correct them before they become full blown issues. They look for ways to make life on their manager easier and less stressful. When they do that they make things better for themselves as well.

Ask yourself one simple question. Who would you prefer to have as an employee? Someone who took up a lot of your time and required your constant attention to handle every little thing, resolve office and personalities disputes and situations or the employee who you rarely had to deal with except when instructions had to be given?

Would you like employees who made your life easier or more complicated?

Would you like employees who added time to your work week or employees who made it possible for you to go home on time most of the days?

If you answered those questions honestly, you will admit that the employees who make life easier for their boss or manager will be the ones who are more appreciated and more highly valued. You will also agree that the employees who make things easier on the manager are far more likely to remain with the company during tough times. After all, if a manager has to cut manpower, the higher maintenance employees are going to be among the first to go.

High maintenance also means keeping your skills and expertise at high levels so you can go about your job performing at a high level without constant interaction from the manager. Adopting a pro-active approach to your job allows the manager to spend their time where their other problems exist and not worrying about you!

How Do I Do This?

Don't create problems. If you do, solve them before they hit the attention of the manager.

Do you best to resolve things before the manager has to, get involved.

If you see a problem starting, solve it quickly before it escalates.

Look for ways to make your manager's life a little bit easier.

Let little stuff slide and don't bother your manager with little things that are just not all that important.

Always look for ways to make things easier, better and cheaper.

Pay attention to deadlines and goals be do your best to meet or beat each one.

Don't wait to be told to do something you already know needs to be done.

Be a Problem Solver

One thing great employees always do is solve problems. They see something that needs to be made better, faster or less costly and they set their minds on making that happen. They look at a problem and instead of leaving the solution up to someone else; they dive in and resolve it themselves. This is a skill that is greatly appreciated by most managers and companies.

Think about everything that can go wrong in a company or an office. Customers can get angry, machines can mal-function, supplies can be late in delivering their products, workplace disputes can cause tension in the office and a myriad of other things can go wrong at a moment's notice.

If you were the manager of that office, your time would be spent constantly addressing issues, solving problems, resolving disputes and handling crises after crises.

You would never really have the time to do the rest of your job because you were spending all your time reacting to the everyday issues of the office.

Great employees help lessen the load. They see something wrong and they will try to fix it. They will go and try to mediate a customer dispute and resolve it instead of just telling the customer to call the manager. They will see the copier is jammed and at least make an attempt to fix it rather than letting it go for someone else to do. If they see two employees involved in a dispute, when appropriate they will try and resolve the situation without anyone else getting involved.

These things are not usually difficult to do. If there are 20 people in an office and each person handles just one or two issues a day that can result in 20-40 fewer situations that the manager has to become involved in! Imagine the workload reduction you would have if someone handled 20 tasks every day for you!

Great employees do not really understand the meaning of the phrase "That's not my job!" Unless there are specific rules or regulations preventing them from doing something, they will proceed without stopping to think whether or not that is considered part of their job description.

Great employees apply a "can do" and proactive attitude when it comes to work.

They see problems as opportunities to make something better. They see problems as challenges and they are always up for that challenge. They rarely ask someone else to do something they are capable of doing themselves. Stop for a minute and think about how valuable that attitude would be in any office.

Great employees also will work together to achieve more difficult or complex issues. Even though the manager might be involved, they will work together with management and share ideas, pitch in when needed and do whatever it takes to resolve the issue or make things better. There is an old saying that goes "Two heads are better than one" which refers to the value in working together and sharing ideas. Well if two heads are better than one, then 5 heads or 20 head are better still!

Which type employee are you? Do you spot a problem and walk away so someone else can take care of it?

Do you spot a problem and wait until it becomes a big problem before doing anything about it?

Are you part of the problem or part of the solution?

Now THAT is something everyone should think about........

How Do I Do This?

Be pro-active. If you see something that needs to be done, DO IT!

Tackle little issues before they become bigger ones.

If within your skill set, at least try to resolve something before getting the manager involved.

Ask other people for help if something appears too difficult.

Always look for ways to make something better, faster or less expensive.

Don't expect others to solve your problems. I would bet that at least a few of them can be solved by a little effort on your part.

Ask yourself if you could do something instead of who you should report the issue to.

Don't be afraid to do more than anyone else. Everyone needs to work together. If you are doing more than everyone else, you can bet someone is noticing that!

Finally, don't ask or expect other people to handle things that you can handle yourself.

Be Assertive & Confident

When it comes to shining in the workplace and being respected by others, one thing stands out as being very desirable in the eyes of management. That is the ability to be assertive and confident. That is because people who are assertive and confident tend to be more productive and influential in the workplace.

Employees who are assertive while not being overbearing are known for being able to drive home what needs to be done and help complete a task or assignment through to completion more effective than those employees who stay in the background and allow others to lead. Great employees are the ones who want to step up and assume the leadership role or make their contributions known. That requires a certain degree of assertiveness.

We have already talked about confidence to some degree but confidence is very important in the workplace. Confidence gives you the ability to believe in yourself and your ideas. Confidence gives you the ability to speak up and be heard whenever you have the chance to contribute and idea, thought, or other contribution.

Confidence also gives us the strength to do more on our own without having to constantly ask questions, seek out approval or advice from the manager of others. Confident people often do more with less input and that results in higher productivity and fewer work stoppages for questions. In general, confident people will take charge and complete more work without needi9ng to involve management and others throughout the process.

Confidence and assertiveness sometimes go hand in hand because the more confident someone is of their abilities, the more they will believe that what they think and do has significant value. This in turn makes us feel valid in speaking up and pushing for what we know in our hearts is the right thing to do.

Contrast that to someone who has limited confidence in their skills or abilities. That person may have doubts in their ability to contribute and because of that stay in the background. They might have very good ideas but are afraid to bring them out in the open. They would be more afraid of fear and ridicule than they would about contributing.

There is nothing wrong with fighting for what you believe in as long as you understand the management structure in the company. If you strongly feel that you have the better idea or suggestion, then great employees will speak up and DISCUSS this with the other people involved.

I say "discuss" because it should be a discussion and not an argument. If you believe your idea or approach is the right one, prepare to state the reasons why your idea is better and give all the benefits the company or manager would receive if your approach is given. Be firm and assertive but not overbearing.

Understand that there will be situations where your idea will not, or cannot be used. IN those situations accept defeat gracefully and move on. No matter what the situation or circumstances, always treat everyone with dignity and respect even if they disagree with you. There is never a valid reason for treating another person with disrespect even if they treat you in that manner.

The only exception for that would involve safety issues. If you have a strong opinion, or if you downright know that something will result in danger to yourself or others, you should make that fear known to the appropriate people. Never allow anything that is dangerous to go unchallenged!

For the majority of situations, your ideas should be shared with your team or manager in an appropriate and respectful manner. If you have a better idea, speak up. If you feel something is a better alternative, speak up. If you see or hear something that isn't right, speak up.

Being able to act in a confident manner helps people feel confident about having you work with them and it inspires confidence in others at the same time. This will help create an overall work environment where the sharing of ideas and thoughts is encouraged.

But I would also caution every employee to monitor the level of assertiveness and confidence that show to others. When someone is so assertive that they run over everyone else in the process, or when others feel threatened by someone else, that can present a great problem. We all have worked with the overbearing person who feels that they are far above everyone else and that no one could possibly have a better idea than they had.

You do not want to be that person. Overbearing or over assertive people stifle the creativity and free flowing of ideas and thoughts within the office or company. You can be confident without being overbearing and obnoxious. You can be assertive when you need to be while still being respectful to others in the workplace.

Sometimes this is a fine balance and in some critical situations there might be a real need for someone to step up and really take charge. IN those cases, you might have to lead with more conviction and force than usual but always remember that this is a special situation and you should revert back to normal when this situation is over or has passed.

How Do I Do This?

Confidence comes from having good skills and education. If your skills or education are weak, improve them by taking classes or gaining experience.

If you have an idea or thought that you feel has merit, speak up and make others aware.

Do not be afraid of having a thought or idea dismissed as wrong. It happens to everyone many times in their lives. You are no exception.

Participate in brain storming sessions. Everyone should get involved. You never know who will come up with the next great idea!

If someone keeps you from speaking up, or if someone intimidates you for some reason, speak to them about it. If they continue to do that, speak to your manager. Chances are if you feel that way someone else feels the same way.

If you see the opportunity to lead, then lead. Leadership experience is something that will be of great use to you in your career and life.

In other words, if you have something to say, go ahead and say it!

Be Committed & Focused

Sometimes it is difficult to remain focused and committed especially when we do the same thing every day. But great employees understand that they play an important role in the overall success and failure of the company and the products and services they create. If any one person should falter in their commitment to excellence and quality, the entire process will suffer!

Employees should view their part of the process as a link in a chain. The entire chain will only be as strong as the weakest link in that chain. So if 20 employees do a great job and one or two do a poor job, then the product or service quality will suffer for everyone.

Imagine if a product is manufactured perfectly, packaged beautifully but shipped to the wrong address because someone made an error with the address.

Or perhaps a 112 pages report is beautifully done and accurately written but two crucial graphs are incorrectly created misrepresenting the value of the product. In either case, a simple task, not done properly, can have a huge impact on the overall result.

The reality of it is that there are no insignificant or valueless jobs. Every task that is done is done for a reason and all those reasons roll up into produces quality products or services. While it might be easy to establish greater value in some of the tasks, it really is true that every employee and every task plays a role in the overall success or failure of the company.

Because of this, it is critical that every employee remain focused on what they are supposed to do and how they are supposed to do it. They should look for ways to constantly improve their performance and improve the quality of the results they produce. Great employees always look for ways to make things better while other employees sometimes find themselves bored and "in a rut" so to speak.

Though it helps to have the company focused on reminding their employee just how important they really are to the company, the primary motivation for improving oneself must always come from within. It is not the company's responsibility to make you improve your skills.

While they might offer to help you regarding that, and even make it easier and cheaper for you to do so, the ultimate responsibility lies with the employees themselves.

Great employees will remain committed and focused towards doing the best job possible. They will not work up to what they are expected to do. Instead, they will work up to the level they expect themselves capable of and that should always exceed what the employer demands or expects. No one was ever fired or disciplined for a doing a better job than was asked! But many people have lost their jobs for performing at a level that was less than expected.

Great employees also focus on the big picture and not their individual roles. They see themselves as part of a team or part of a company that produces excellent quality products and services. They take pride in what the company produces and they take pride in their role in that process. While individual awards and recognition are always nice and appreciated, great employees also take pride in what their teams and companies accomplish.

It is sometimes easy to lose focus these days with everything that goes on around us. But those employees who can remain focused and dedicated to doing the very best they can will develop a closer and more valuable relationship with management and have a much more secure and financially rewarding career in the future.

How Do I Do This?

Know your role with the company and what you help accomplish. Take pride in the end result of what you helped make or create.

Try and understand what you do and why it is necessary. The more value we attach to what we do the more we will become committed to it.

Always demand more of yourself than what others demand of you. That way you will never disappoint anyone other than yourself.

Always look for ways to improve your skills, expertise and knowledge. It is much better to be more qualified than less qualified.

Always concentrate on what you need to do in order to make something better. You can only control what you do and contribute.

Do your best each and every day.

Be Reliable

Ok, this one is easy. Being reliable and being able to be counted upon to do what is assigned or expected of you is one character trait that every single manager and company looks for in their employees. No one wants someone they hope will show up, they want someone they KNOW will show up!

Sometimes it seems that being on time and reliable has become one of those things that just aren't important anymore. It seems that more and more people show up late or not at all and other people do whatever they feel like whenever they feel like it. I'm not sure why this has happened but it creates problems for everyone else involved.

Employees have responsibilities in their jobs. They are expected to do their jobs and complete their tasks and assignments on time. They are supposed to work together to achieve common goals and to make the office or work environment less stressful and peaceful.

This can only happen when everyone is on board and does what they are supposed to do when they are supposed to do it.

It's easy to be reliable. Anyone can do it. All it takes is a little commitment and a little bit of consideration for the other people in your life or office. With that in mind, here are a few ways you can become known as a very reliable person or employee:

Be on Time

If you say you are going to be somewhere by a certain time, be there at the stated time. In fact, it is a good practice to always arrive 10-15 minutes early to allow for travel problems or other unforeseen circumstances.

If something happens that prevents you from being on time, like car trouble, an accident on the freeway or a mass transit issue, then use your cell phone or home phone and notify the people you are supposed to meet. It is also a good policy to get the contact numbers of everyone you have to meet just for situations like these. You should always be aware that other people have schedules as well and when you are late you make them late for future appointments as well.

As for the office, if your shift starts at 8AM, be there at 8AM. Not 8:15 or 8:30 or whenever you feel like it.

Not only does this reflect poorly on you but it creates problems with the other people in the office. They will wonder why it is all right for you to come in late when they are there on time. It is also disrespectful to other who commit to being there on time.

The same thing holds true for office meetings. If the meeting is scheduled for 9AM, be there at 9AM. Do not make everyone wait while you take "just one more call" or hit the coffee station. It is rude and disrespectful of others.

Be Honest

If you say something, make sure it is correct and truthful as you know it. If you are not sure if something is true, keep it to yourself and do some research before repeating it. Gossip and false statements can cause a lot of problems within the office and for employees and the company. Make sure you are certain before you say something.

Do not lie to avoid responsibility or blame for anything. Always be honest and up front with everything you do. If you make a mistake, own up to it. If you say you will do something and you didn't do it, own up to it and let people know why. Do not run and hide from your responsibilities.

Do What You Say

If you make a commitment to do something, do it. If you say you will do something or take care of something, do it. People need to take other peoples word for most things. They need to depend on you and that what you say is what is going to happen.

Most of the time larger projects will depend on many people each doing their own part by a specific deadline. If one or more people do not do what they are supposed to do by that deadline, the entire project can come to a screeching halt!

Do what you say, when you say you will do it. When something comes up that may prevent you from following through on your commitments, talk to the people involved and explain what happened so they can adjust what they have to do and still feel that you are a reliable person at heart.

Do What Needs to Be Done

We have said this so many times in other parts of this book but it bears repeating again because this is such a crucial part of being a great employee. You need to be thought of as someone who can be relied on to help get things done and make things happen. Other employees and management must feel that if something comes up in your area that you are the one who can be counted upon to take care of the problem or report it to someone who can resolve it.

That means stepping up and taking responsibility for something even when it might not be the easy or popular thing to do. It means taking care of something even though it might mean staying a little later or coming in a bit earlier to see that something is ready when it is needed. Companies are full of people who stand back and let other people step up and do what is needed. Do not be one of those people. Be one of the ones who do what is needed when it is needed.

Follow Through

Reliable people take ownership of situations. Great employees will not only recognize a problem, but they will make sure it is resolved and follow the process through until everything is complete.

That might mean seeing a problem, informing the right people about it, and then monitoring the progress until everything has been resolved. Many employees wash their hands of things once they report it to someone else. But instead of walking away and leaving something to someone else, monitor what happens after you report it to make sure everything is being done that should be done.

In many cases the follow-up after reporting is more important than the incident itself.

Remember that many people have many projects and tasks to manage at the same time. Things do get lost in the shuffle or put on the back burner and left there. Follow through and remind people when things need to happen or get done.

Pay Attention to Deadlines

Deadlines are usually there for a reason even though we might not understand the reasons behind them. But in business rarely is a project the work of just one person. While it even might seem that way, someone else needs the project, or your part of the project, done by a specific time so other things can move forward.

Just doing something is usually not good enough. You need to complete the task by the time it is needed if not before. Great employees respect deadlines and work hard to adhere to them. If something happens that prevents a deadline from being met, then the employee should contact the other people involved as soon as they realize the issue. Do not hide from deadlines do you best o meet or beat them.

How Do I Do This?

If you say you will do something, then do it.

If you make a commitment, keep it.

If you are expected somewhere by a certain time, be there 10-15 minutes early.

If there is an assigned deadline, manage your time so that you meet or beat that deadline.

Keep others informed of delays or changes in status as quickly as possible.

Always be honest and tell the truth.

Do things without being asked when the situation calls for it.

Get a reputation as being someone who can be depended and counted upon at all times.

Help others with their deadlines or tasks without seeking recognition or credit.

Be Pro-Active

Depending on who you are and how you go through your life, this one is either going to be the easiest or most difficult thing you will have to do. It involves changing not only how you do things, but how you see them and how you perform them. It sometimes involves a complete shift in the way we look at how we go through life. The good news is that once we make the change in attitude, our lives automatically become easier and far less stressful!

Simply put, being pro-active means going ahead and doing things before they really need to be done. For some of us that might be strange. After all, there is so much to do, and so little time, why would we do something that wasn't even due yet? While that is a good question at times, the answer is a very simple one.

When we do things before they are required to be done, we can exercise more control over the entire process. We can schedule things on our schedule and avoid being pressured to jam 2 days or work into 1 day because of a looming deadline. We can drastically reduce "all nighter" work sessions and replace them with more controlled and efficient standard workdays. Plus, we will be more able to provide our minds and bodies the rest they both need to function at their best.

For some people, having a task due on Friday means starting it on Thursday or even Friday morning. After all, if something takes 4 hours to do, you should easily be able to complete it in an 8 hour day, right?

Of course you should. Unless something else comes up that takes you away from your scheduled work. Or unless the servers go down or your computer crashes. Or unless you catch the stomach virus or the flu. Or unless the information or other things you need for your task arrive later than expected. Or unless a huge snowstorm or other weather event closes business for the day.

But those things never, ever happen. Right??????

As an employee, your goal should be to get everything done as quickly as possible while still maintaining excellent quality and accuracy. That means scheduling tasks as quickly as possible even if they are not due for quite a while.

Naturally anything that requires time specific information such as reports and other item might not be able to be done early but most other things can.

For example, if you have to create a cover graphic and it is due in two weeks, if you have time to do it this week, then do it this week. This way it is done and if anything should come up within the next two weeks it will not matter because your graphic is already done! If you wait 12 days before you start on it and you should get sick or something else pops up, you could find yourself in trouble.

Managers love pro-active employees because they have a much better track record when it comes to getting more done in less time. Other employees like pro-active employees because it helps them get more done as well. When more things are ready earlier, it makes life easier on everyone!

Speaking about making life easier, people who live life on a pro-active basis have less stress in their lives as well. They complete more tasks and project far ahead of schedule so they are not subject to the last minute pressures like everyone else is. They are able to work more on their schedule and when it is convenient to them instead of working on someone else's schedule.

Control is the whole point. Even if the task or assignment will take the exact same amount of time to complete, isn't it better to spend the time on your schedule than someone else's?

If you have to work two nights in order to complete a project, wouldn't it be better for YOU to choose the nights when you had fewer things to do? Of course it would!

Being pro-active lets you assume more of the control over situations. You control them, they do not control you! Even when something does control you it is much better when you only have one or two things controlling you instead of 7 or 8! Being pro-active means exercising more control over what you do and how you do it.

Being pro-active also has another benefit as well. When you address things, especially problems, earlier, you get to resolve them faster as well. Which usually means the problem or situation has not been around as long and its impact has not been as great as it could have been. So problems and issues are easier to solve, with less effort and far less stress.

So now we know that being pro-active makes life easier, more productive and far less stressful. We also know that being pro-active allows us to exercise more control over what we do and how we do it. We also know that being pro-active allows us to work when it is better for us while still getting more done in less time.

Since we now know all the benefits, is there possibly any reason why being pro-active is not something everyone should be doing? Is there any valid reason for making life more difficult and stressful than it could be?

No, there isn't.

How Do I Do This?

Schedule any jobs, tasks or responsibilities as soon as you can. Don't put off until tomorrow what you can easily do today!

Keep a list of what needs to be done. Sort it by deadlines and priorities. Create monthly, weekly and daily lists.

Build time into your schedule to account for last minute requests and problems.

Handle problems and issue when they are first encountered and are small. Do not let something wait until it grows into a real problem.

Play an active role in getting things done in the office or workplace. More gets accomplished in less time when everyone works together.

If you see something needs to be done and you are capable of doing it, just do it.

If you see a potential problem or issue, bring it to someone's attention now. Do not wait until a problem actually happens.

Look for ways to make things better now before a problem arises.

If you can do something now that will make something better in the future, then do it!

Be Positive

Ok, this one is an easy one. When you come to work every day, come with a smile on your face. Adopt a positive attitude when it comes to work and your role in it. Even if things are not going well at work, understand that a positive attitude will actually help make things better for everyone.

As we said before, not everything goes right in life. The workplace is no different. Problems will always arise, people will always have problems with each other and things will need to be done that no one either wants to do or sees the reasons for. Nothing we can do can stop this so we just need to learn how to deal with these things a little better when they come along.

People always have a choice when it comes to how they react to something. They can either dwell on the negatives and complain about everything that is wrong or they can look for the good that often accompanies negative things.

In other words, we can choose to either look for the silver lining or ignore it. The choice is ours.

From the management perspectives, a positive employees is an employee who "gets it" and wants to do good work and help be part of the teams overall success. Positive employees are usually committed to making things better and for taking negative situations or problems and resolving them quickly and with better results. Employees with this type of attitude are known for being high producers, valued teammates and have a much more secure future with the company.

On the flip side, employees who spend most of their time complaining or finding fault with everything are not looked at very highly by management. Management is not looking for people who complain about things. They are look for people who find something wrong and then do something about it. They are not looking for people who complain, find fault and then just walk away.

The great thing about having a positive attitude is that usually something bad has something good that can be taken from it. A problem with a piece of machinery, for example, might result in a redesign that makes the machine faster and more reliable. A common problem with a piece of software could result in a new design that has more features and is far more stable.

A customer problem could shed light on a problem with a company policy that could be changed and result in much better customer satisfaction.

The list could go on and on but all of those examples share a common factor. When you search for a solution and look at everything from a positive point of view, good things usually happen. When something breaks for the 5th time you can either say the machine is a pile of junk and walk away or you can look more closely and design a better part that will outlast the original. Then when production increases the machine will work without problems in the future.

Or that problem with the policy that really angered the customer? You might dive into that problem and find an outdated policy that you can retool to make things much faster and much better for the customer. Or you could just complain that all policies suck and not do a damned thing.

As I said before, it's your choice.

The fact is, positive people are in much more demand and have a higher value to the company than their negative counterparts. Right there that should be a good enough reason for anyone to change how they look at things at work. But positive people also experience much more satisfaction, take part in much more success and become a more vital part of the company's workforce.

The usually progress up the ranks much faster than their negative counterparts and that usually results in more money and more prestige.

So right now you have a decision to make. Are you going to be a negative person or a positive person? Whatever you decide, the choice is yours.

Just be positive about it..............

How Do I Do This?

The next time something negative or bad occurs, force yourself to look for the good in it.

Look for a solution first and complain about it later.

Don't give in to a problem. Instead work it through, find the issue, and kick its butt to the curb!

Replace the frown with a smile. For some reason, it's hard to be negative when you are smiling!

Always look for some way to make something better than it currently is.

Ask yourself "How Can I?" not "Why Should I?"

Be a Team Player

This is the last character trait and we saved it for last because it is one of the most important traits any employee can have. A strong argument could be made for it being the most important trait. The ability to work well with others and become a real team player is one of the cornerstones of a well run office or company. Those who learn to thrive in a culture where everyone works together accomplish far more in less time than when people work independently.

Most well run offices work so well because everyone in the office works together as a team. There is a "blurring" of roles and responsibilities and people just concentrate on getting things done instead of who technically is supposed to do what. In other words, people have each other's back whenever possible.

Being known as a team player is important because it signifies you as being someone who is more concerned with the overall success of the team than you are in personal success and recognition. Team players work together while individual often work against each other competing for recognition, praise and credit. That kind of attitude creates an "Everyone for themselves" environment where everyone is out for themselves and no one else.

That kind of situation often results in back stabbing, in-fighting and an overall lack of cooperation between most people in the office. Projects get stalled, deadlines get blown out of the water and more time is spent deciding who is going to get the credit instead of getting more accomplished.

Great employees learn to work together to achieve a common goal. They understand that it is better to work well with others and to help others whenever needed. This generates a close relationship between employees and makes them work even closer and harder to achieve goals, meet deadlines, and produce better results.

Placing personal gain and success behind the good of the entire team is an important part of being a team player. Though this might seem contrary to doing things that will make you look good in the eyes of management, being a team player is something that management looks upon very highly.

They will notice those who function well within a team and understand that those individual are putting the company and the team above their own goals.

Great employees also understand that working well with others encourages all employees to share their skills and expertise so that everyone becomes more knowledge and productive. This leads to cross training situation where everyone learns how to do multiple jobs within the office.

This can come in really handy whenever someone takes a vacation, calls in sick or otherwise needs to take time off. In a team environment, someone else will step in and perform those job responsibilities. That leads to less pressure and stress and makes it more likely that the company and office will be able to better make it through any personnel issues in the future.

From the employee's point of view, being an integral part of a team has personal benefits as well. Employees who worked more closely together share knowledge and experiences and the result is that all employees learn more and become more highly skilled as a result. This opens up opportunities for them down the road and makes them more valuable in the marketplace at the same time.

In a team environment each employee's strengths are used for the betterment of everyone.

This allows each employee to excel at what they do best while everyone reaps the rewards of a job well done. The result is less stress, better results and an overall improvement in the workplace environment.

Last, but certainly not least is the economic reality of becoming a team player. Though it might be hard to accept, things are changing in the workplace. Fewer people are being expected to handle more work in the same amount of time they had before. That means people must either find new ways of accomplishing existing workload or they must work longer hours or take longer to get things done.

Taking longer is usually an unacceptable option and people can only work longer hours for a limited time before results and quality suffer. So the remaining option, finding different ways of accomplishing tasks is really the only viable option. Working as a team is one of those options. Employees who are able to work closely with each other as part of a team are going to be the employees that make this transition into the future.

Teamwork is a skill that must be learned and must be practiced. But the rewards are well worth the effort and every employee should embrace teamwork as a way to get more done with less stress and less pressure. Great employees do this and employees looking to become great will learn this valuable skill.

How Do I Do This?

Be helpful to fellow employees and help out when needed.

Do not wait to be asked, offer your help and assistance.

Create an environment where everyone works together and allows everyone to use their individual skills for the common good.

Share your knowledge and expertise with a co-worker.

Train each other to do each other's jobs.

Place your personal gain behind the gain and success of the team.

Conclusion

Being an employee for some companies is not a walk in the park. But if you have the right attitude, and understand the relationship between the company and its employees, you can become very successful with a great chance for advancement. That is exactly what we have tried to teach you throughout this book.

We also realize that some parts of this book appeared to favor the employer instead of the employee. We do not apologize for that because that is the reality of the situation in most cases. The employer controls who is hired and fired and that's just reality. But there is good news as well.

The great majority of companies value their good employees. They understand that their future is controlled not just by management but by the employees who produce the products and services the company produces. Without their employees, there would be no products and no services.

Good companies understand this and respect the employees who do a good job for them.

So the employee does have significant control over their success within the company. They have the ability to greatly influence their role and future with the company by the things they do day in and day. If they exceed expectations, they will do well. If they have the right attitude, they will do well. If they can work well with others they will do well.

Throughout this book we have covered many concepts, behaviors and attitudes of what we feel represent the perfect employee. Some, if not most, of these things you probably already do each and every day. If that is the case, that's great! If you don't do most of these things already then it's time to start!

The great thing is that every single concept or attitude we discussed in this book can be easily integrated into anyone's life. You don't need fancy education or a wealth of experience. All you need is the willingness to change your behavior. And you should care about what you are doing and why you are doing it.

There, we've finally said it. You need to care about what you are doing if you want to be successful. No book can teach you how to be successful or better at something if you don't care or give a damn about something.

But if you care about something, if you really want to do your best, then the sky's the limit to your success.

If you actually made it this far into the book, I believe you really do care about your job and career. If you didn't, you would have closed the book a couple of hours ago and flipped on the television. But the fact that you are here, at the end of the book, means you found some value in what you have read and how it possibly relates to you and your situation.

So that already gives you an advantage over a lot of people working out there today. You are not someone who punches a clock and waits for quitting time. You are someone who takes pride in what you do and how you do it. For people like you, the future is bright. Very bright.

Employers want people like you and once they find you, they will not want you to leave. They will help you grow within the company and share in your success. And if for some reason your company doesn't treat their employees in that fashion, there are many companies out there that will.

It all comes down to caring and attitude. If you care about what you are doing and why you do it, and you have the right attitude, everything else falls into place. You will want to get the best skills and those skills will take you further. You will want to perform at a high level and people who perform at the highest levels get the most opportunities and promotions.

Last, but certainly not least, is that great employees are secure employees. Great employees show their value every single day. Companies know they need to hold on to their best employees no matter what the economy or industry conditions are at the moment. In today's marketplace, job security and peace of mind is a wonderful thing to have and most people envy those who have it.

So right now we have a decision to make. We can follow some of the advice and concepts in this book or we can go on doing what we have been doing for the last few years. That is your decision and no one can make it for you. You have to decide what is right for you and then you need to go out and do it!

The thing about change is that YOU must lead the change. If you change nothing, nothing changes. If you keep the old behavior you are not likely to get different or better results!

So go back through the book and pick out a couple of concepts or ideas that you feel will give you the best "return" on your efforts. Pick out what you feel will give you the greatest impact in the least amount of time. Don't try and change everything at once. Just one or two things at a time. Once those become habits and no longer require your thoughts and effort you can move on to the next two changes.

Don't try and do too much at once. Slow and steady always beat crash and burn. Do things in a slow and controlled manner that you can control and monitor. If something doesn't work the way you thought it would, don't give up. Make a minor change and try again.

Your own attitude and performance will dictate how your future rolls out. So do yourself a favor and make a commitment today to work on your tomorrow. If you can do that and stick with it, you will become a great employee with a bright and secure future!

Made in the USA
Las Vegas, NV
19 December 2022